A LIFE OF LIVING PRAYER
It Is All Prayer

Dawn A. Sweet

Copyright © 2014 Dawn A. Sweet.

All rights reserved. No part of this book may be used or reproduced by any means, graphic, electronic, or mechanical, including photocopying, recording, taping or by any information storage retrieval system without the written permission of the publisher except in the case of brief quotations embodied in critical articles and reviews.

WestBow Press books may be ordered through booksellers or by contacting:

WestBow Press
A Division of Thomas Nelson & Zondervan
1663 Liberty Drive
Bloomington, IN 47403
www.westbowpress.com
1 (866) 928-1240

Because of the dynamic nature of the Internet, any web addresses or links contained in this book may have changed since publication and may no longer be valid. The views expressed in this work are solely those of the author and do not necessarily reflect the views of the publisher, and the publisher hereby disclaims any responsibility for them.

Any people depicted in stock imagery provided by Thinkstock are models, and such images are being used for illustrative purposes only.
Certain stock imagery © Thinkstock.

Scriptures taken from the Holy Bible, New International Version®, NIV®. Copyright © 1973, 1978, 1984, 2011 by Biblica, Inc.™ Used by permission of Zondervan. All rights reserved worldwide. www.zondervan.com The "NIV" and "New International Version" are trademarks registered in the United States Patent and Trademark Office by Biblica, Inc.™ All rights reserved.

Revised Standard Version of the Bible, copyright 1952 [2nd edition, 1971] by the Division of Christian Education of the National Council of the Churches of Christ in the United States of America. Used by permission. All rights reserved.

New Revised Standard Version Bible, copyright 1989, Division of Christian Education of the National Council of the Churches of Christ in the United States of America. Used by permission. All rights reserved.

ISBN: 978-1-4908-6333-7 (sc)
Library of Congress Control Number: 2015900540

Printed in the United States of America.

WestBow Press rev. date: 01/07/2015

*This book is dedicated to
Thomas R. McKibbens
who truly lives a life
of living prayer.*

FOREWORD

In the tradition of Brother Lawrence, Julian of Norwich, Teresa of Avila, and Thomas R. Kelly, comes Dawn Sweet: except Dawn Sweet is a contemporary Protestant who remains within the Baptist Tradition! She is not the sole voice among Baptists who ponder the life of prayer, but she is definitely lonely. Baptists generally draw heavily on the frontier tradition of prayer inspired in the moment. Contemplative prayer, especially written prayers, are not easily found among that particular wing of the Protestant world.

But as a Baptist, Dawn inherits the great legacy of Roger Williams: namely, soul liberty. She has immersed herself (a good Baptist verb) in the life of prayer, and she shares it with us who read this profoundly moving book. Like many of the great devotional classics, it is not long in pages; it is long in meaning. As Dawn would say, it is long on "pondering." "Ponder" is one of her favorite words, and you can see why when you read this book. It is not a book to rush through; it takes pondering, reflecting, brooding, and digesting. To read this book well is not a race to the finish line, but a lingering walk among the hues and colors of the life of prayer.

Dawn Sweet draws a clear distinction between a person's prayer life and a person's life of prayer. She opts for the latter, for prayer is not seen here as separate from the rest of life. It is not a room set apart, but a whole house of prayer. In short and thoughtful chapters, she guides us through places, symbols, actions, and the language of prayer. Hers is a guidebook for people who want to grow deeper into the life of prayer. She closes the book with powerful, poetic and moving prayers which she has written. They, like the prose chapters, are to be read with care and reflection.

This is a book to be kept close at hand, and one hopes that it will not be the last published writing from this sensitive follower of Christ.

Thomas R. McKibbens

Thomas R. McKibbens has served as both pastor and seminary professor during the last thirty years. He has taught at Harvard Divinity School, Boston University School of Theology, and Andover Newton Theological School. He is the author of two books one being <u>The Forgotten Heritage, A Lineage of Great Baptist Preachers</u> as well as numerous articles in theological and historical journals. However, his priority is his work in the local church where he brings his gifts of preaching, praying, sensitivity and compassion to all whom he pastors.

PREFACE

Growing up in a Christian family and the church I thought I knew the meaning of prayer and I actually did but at the same time didn't. It meant to talk with God, not just to him but with him. As time went on I discerned that that was only one step in communion with him through prayer.

I remember as a teen-ager attending the mid-week prayer meeting and the attendees would pray in length concerning their family, the church, missionaries and whatever else was on their heart and mind. Then there would be the up dating of the prayer list, which should be kept currant. However, at the conclusion I would question and ask isn't there more to a life of prayer?

As I began to experience new paths on my journey I kept questioning the philosophy of prayer and how it coincided with the teachings of Jesus and the scriptures. Jesus prayed and as I began to understand more of his teachings I realized his life was one of living prayer. It wasn't just being alone with his Father and teaching his disciples to say the "The Lord's Prayer" it was his parables, miracles, his moment by moment living.

I was called to do interim work at a near by church and the first Sunday I was there I found a very long prayer list on the pulpit and I asked how is this meaningfully incorporated in worship? The reply was "read it." I smiled, but thought oh no. It was not only long, but several of the names were not easily pronounced and not knowing exactly how to pronounce names is not being respectful of the person and also takes away from the prayer. After a few weeks of poorly reading this list I inquired as to who these people actually were and to why they were on the list. As it turned out several of the people were not known nor was the reason they or others were being prayed for. The list shrunk greatly and eventually became all inclusive in the pastoral prayer. Prayers can be stumbling blocks and bumps in the road if not prepared in a sensitive thoughtful manner. They can even detract from heart felt and Christ centered worship.

As children we learned to pray kneeling down by our beds prior to being tucked in and given the good night and sleep well kiss. We also prayed before and maybe even after meals depending upon our tradition. At holiday time everyone was impressed with the words (memorized from a little Golden Book) that we quoted to give thanks. We even dared to ask God to give us an "A" on a test we hadn't sufficiently studied for and we would ask him to bless everyone we could bring to mind including the family pet (s). Eventually we memorized the prayers of the church, probably beginning with "The Lord's Prayer." I say memorize for that is most likely what it was, memorization. Did someone explain it to us phrase by phrase by making it contemporary, how we were to apply it to our daily living, inform us how it originated and why it is prayed throughout the Christian world? Probably it was not.

As my journey with prayer continued I realized I had only just begun. Prayer is so much more than I realized, it is not just talking with God, it is total communion with him. Reading I Thessalonians 5:17(NIV), where Paul is instructing the Christian community to "Pray continually" I pondered over and over again how can I strive towards such a goal? My answer came slowly as I was guided to read the writings of the mystics of another age, church fathers and mothers, Thomas Merton, Henri Nouwen, and numerous other contemplative writers.

As my life of living prayer began to develop my total concept of prayer began to change and continues to as I strive to live a life of prayer. If we live centered in Jesus the Christ and commit to follow his teachings we then are working towards continuous prayer. Unceasing prayer is communion with God. God is within and around us, his presence is constant.

> Prayer is communion with God.
> It is talking with him.
> It is listening with him.
> It is following and working with him.
> It is living with him.

Formal prayer, how we utilize silence, the way we live, and the way we work is all prayer. They are interconnected because all is connected to God through his love. Saint Benedict, author of the Benedictine Rule, taught that if we are centered in God whether formal prayer or work it is all prayer. Sister Ann Lee of the Shaker tradition also believed, if our hearts are in tune with God our work with our hands is for him. This is living prayer, for how we pray is how we live and how we live is how we pray.

Through my experience of slowly gaining understanding of living prayer I was given the desire to share this with others who had come to the threshold of wanting a deeper communion with God through unceasing prayer. I have facilitated retreats, seminars and dialogue groups for several years and through these means I have witnessed many blessings. Not only do the participants grow in their awareness of his presence and unceasing prayer, but so do I. Some have testified that this direction and acceptance of it has enriched and blessed their Christian journey and has given them a solid foundation through times of anxious struggle and times of true joy as well.

This book would not be possible without all of those who took the step to grow into and through a life of living prayer. The names are too numerous to list but you know who you are and I extend my sincere prayer of thank you. I do particularly offer a prayer of thanksgiving for the Rev. Philip D. Goff who encouraged me to write a book publishing my prayers, some of which are included in this book and the Rev. Dr. Thomas R. McKibbens whose friendship, mentoring and believing in my ministry has given me the confidence to share my ministry through this writing. Thanksgiving is also extended to the Sisters and Brothers at the Saint Scholastica Priory and Saint Mary's Monastery in Petersham, Massachusetts for the quiet space to pray, ponder, and to write as well as experience their abundant welcoming spirit. I also offer a prayer of thanksgiving for all who have supported me in so many ways through my ministry and writing.

Petersham, Massachusetts
Summer, 2014   Dawn A. Sweet

A SPECIAL PLACE

"Very early in the morning, while it was still dark, Jesus got up, left the house and went off to a solitary place, where he prayed. Simon and his companions went to look for him, and when they found him, they exclaimed: 'Everyone is looking for you! Jesus replied, 'Let us go somewhere else to the nearby village, so I can preach, there also. That is why I came.'"
Mark 1:35-38 (NIV)

"To create a special corner or space in our home can be extremely helpful, a place that simply speaks out and reminds us to leave the busy avenues."

It is difficult to find a time and a place to be with Jesus so to quietly commune with him. We let an over abundance of clutter and traffic get in the way. So much seems so important to us, our days get filled with stress, frustration and fatigue and if we would only learn to take some necessary time with him in our "cell" those feelings would at least ease.

To create a special corner or space in our home can be extremely helpful, a place that simply speaks out and reminds us to leave the busy avenues. It can be very simple. Choose a place where we can sit in comfort, with possibly a small table where we can place our Bible, contemplative and inspirational books, possibly a candle or some other symbol that keeps us focused on our time apart from the crowded schedule to feel his constant presence and to commune with him. Each time we see or walk by this special place, we are reminded that we need to throw the calendar and clock away and give our time over to him in moments to talk with and listen with him.

The duration of time is secondary to the quality of the time. The quality of the time alone with him in our cell (our place set apart) will be visible when we are working with him out of the cell (in our community of faith and beyond).

Jesus taught us to be alone with him as he was with his Father, but even he was alone he also taught us that he had to go and use his gifts, to share with his neighbors – "Go to the village." (Mark 1: 38 paraphrase DAS)

This is where the journey begins in a life of living prayer. The conscious commitment and discipline to find a place apart and to abandon all distractions around us is not easy, but needed. It even takes prayer to begin the closer walk with him.

PRAYER OF EXAMINATION

*"Create in me a clean heart, O God, and put
a new and right spirit within me."*
Psalm 51:10 (RSV)

*"Through examination we are more able to receive
and appreciate his grace and mercy."*

After we have found, created and organized our place apart, the next step is to truly and honestly commune with God through a prayer of examination. If we do not pause and examine our day by day living, we will not grow in our life of living prayer. If we do not discipline ourselves to carefully inventory our journey we will simply be treading water and lose our focus of praying unceasingly.

We need to ask ourselves if we treat our neighbor according to the teachings of Jesus. How often do we put ourselves before his vision and mission? Each day we need to examine and find where we fall short. Through this prayer of examination we get to know our self and be more ken to the community we worship, live, work and spend time in fellowship. Keeping in mind how we pray is how we live and how we live is how we pray.

We must first go to our special place, our place apart and become calm and quiet, by listening to peaceful music, reading scripture, a prayer or a short passage from a book or just simply be. We begin by offering a prayer of thanksgiving and then slowly with him examine our living, not only where did I fall short, but be open to identify where we did truly work with him and treated our neighbor justly through humility and love. After the prayer of examination we continue our time with him as we feel led with prayer, reading, thought and pondering.

Through examination we are more able to receive and appreciate his grace and mercy. We must always remember that this is a journey with him, a journey of learning, a journey of growing, and a journey of giving.

PRAYING THE HOURS

"Several times a day I praise you for your righteous law."
Psalm 119:164 (NIV)

"Mary did not choose the life of a religious, but she did choose to focus on Jesus and that is what is necessary."

Religious orders pray what is called the Liturgy of the Hours or the Divine Office. These times vary amongst religious orders. However, they all begin very early in the morning, some as early as 3:00 AM. Their day also concludes rather early in the evening around 8:00 or 8:30 PM. They prayerfully enter the chapel generally seven times a day and pray the hours and also celebrate the Eucharist. These liturgical hours are based on certain points of the day; early morning, mid-morning, midday, mid - afternoon, evening prayer and night prayer. This praying generally consists of psalms, canticles and antiphons, the Our Father, the Gloria, the Kyrie, scripture, the doxology and a hymn. There are a few moments of examination and at Compline (the last hour or completion of the day) some orders include the Nunc Dimittis (Song of Simeon from Luke 2:29-32). Then there is a hymn sung to pay homage to the Blessed Virgin Mary and the hour is concluded with the sprinkling of holy water as a blessing given by the Superior in the name of God.

We of course cannot comply to such a schedule, however we can become mindful of his presence throughout the day as we make our life one of living prayer. We need to keep in mind that prayer is not just words, it is silence and action as well. I would venture to say that most of our prayers are action if we feed ourselves well in our place apart with prayers of silence and words.

The Benedictine brothers and sisters follow the Rule of Saint Benedict which he authored around 530 AD (exact date is not known) and they believe that all they do is prayer. When they work out-of-doors, prepare meals, create works of art or eatable products such as cheese, fruit cake, jam, chocolates etc. (which is done for financial assistance), pray the hours, study or greet people seeking time to hear that "still small voice," it is all prayer.

The monks at Saint Joseph's Abbey in Spencer, Massachusetts are Cistercian "Trappist" monks, but follow the Rule of Saint Benedict. A few of them make pottery and among their creations are jugs of various shapes, sizes and colors. make pottery and among their creations are jugs of various shapes, sizes and colors. Realizing they recognize their work as prayer, I have called these jugs prayer jugs and the people who have received them are reminded of prayer in various ways. Some carry the very small ones with them in a pocket and each time they touch it they are reminded of living prayer and God's presence. Others glance at them and can vision the infinite number of prayers that are living in their jugs.

I have spent an extended time in a priory – monastery and this experience has given me a sensitivity and appreciation of the litany and a deeper awareness of the liturgical hours. Words echoed frequently begin with, "God come to my assistance make haste to help me."(Psalm 70:1 a biblical paraphrase) "Then Glory be to the Father and to the Son and to the Holy Spirit. As it was in the beginning is now and ever shall be" is frequently chanted as well as the Kyrie: "Lord, have mercy, Christ, have mercy, Lord, have mercy" these powerful words which are rooted in scripture come to mind frequently throughout the day and remind me of his omnipresence.

Praying the hours is like the story of Mary and Martha. Martha being disturbed by Mary listening to Jesus and not helping her prepare the meal. Jesus said to Martha, "you are worried and upset about many things, but only one thing is needed. Mary has chosen what is better and it will not be taken away from her." (Luke 10:41 NIV)

Mary did not choose the life of a religious, but she did choose to focus on Jesus and that is what is necessary, just as he told Martha. When we place and keep our focus on him that is praying unceasingly through words, silence and action and in that way we are living a liberal – free awareness of the hours, for his presence is always with us, we just need to be aligned with him and aware of the intensity of his peace and love shrouding us.

SYMBOLS OF OUR FAITH

"I am the vine; you are the branches. If a man remains in me and I in him, he will bear much fruit; apart from me you can do nothing."
John 15:5 (NIV)

"Prayer does indeed not only represent but demonstrates how we pray is how we live and how we live is how we pray."

We enter our churches and will most likely see a cross or in some traditions a crucifix. There possibly could be an open Bible, candles, an altar and the table of remembrance, a baptistry or baptismal font. There may also be icons, statues, pictures, carvings and stained glass windows that portray symbols of our faith.

During Advent most churches exhibit an Advent Wreath and offer various readings and/or hymns as the candles of hope, peace, joy and love are lighted during the four weeks of Advent and then on Christmas Eve and/or day we witness the lighting of the Christ candle.

For Palm Sunday we have palms and on Easter the flowers, especially the white lilies have become a symbol of new life. Some traditions have also adopted the butterfly as a symbol of the resurrection.

Today more and more communities of faith are sharing the experience of ashes on Ash Wednesday, inviting people to be more conscious of the forty days of repentance, examination and a life of unceasing living prayer.

On Maundy Thursday the Eucharist is the central symbol and on Good Friday the altar is stripped and frequently covered with black to await the white of purity on Easter morn.

The liturgical colors are displayed from the altar, pulpit and lectern to guide us through the Christian year. The green which is used in ordinary time, I like to reflect upon as a time to grow from the "feeding" of the fuller seasons of Advent, Lent, Easter and Pentecost. Green represents growth as in plant life. The white signifies Christ's purity, purple his majesty and red the fire of Pentecost, the coming of the Holy Spirit. The pastors often, but not always, wear stoles that coordinate in color with the paraments, but even if the colors don't coordinate, the stoles still have a very significant meaning.

The stole is a symbol of servanthood, work and the sharing of the word of God. When Jesus washed his disciple's feet at the Passover Feast – the Lord's Supper, it is said that he used a cloth, possibly from around his neck.

The coming to the table of remembrance, thanksgiving and prayer is the most poignant of all and I will share more on this in a future chapter.

Not only are there symbols in our house of worship, but in our homes. Objects and art work that we carefully choose to remind us of our Christian journey, how we should pray and how we should live. They are symbols of prayer and possibly the one who designed or made these symbols believed as the Shakers, "hands to work and hearts to God."

Not only do we have tangible symbols we have the parables and lessons taught by Jesus using much symbolism. Vines and branches, camels and needles, lamps and stands, bread and wine, water and light, seeds and weeds, solid ground and shaky sand and many many more examples, but when we hear or read these words our mind's eye creates visuals and they become symbols of our belief and our life of living prayer.

How we live our life and treat our neighbor is a symbol of our beliefs, commitment and journey. Prayer does indeed represent, but demonstrates that how we pray is how we live and how we live is how we pray. Jesus' life, his living, was symbolic of how we must pray and live.

There are symbols all around us and that moves us on to our next chapter, "Prayer Walks."

PRAYER WALKS

*"He has showed you, O man, what is good. And what
does the Lord require of you? To act justly and to
love mercy and to walk humbly with your God."*
Micah 6:8 (NIV)

*"Whether we choose a wooded path, a neighborhood street, a
park, a mountain trail, a labyrinth or a full blown pilgrimage
walk, they are all prayer in communication with our Creator."*

It is a known fact that walking, especially in and with what God created relieves stress. Just think if we did prayer walks how much stress we could diminish in our lives. There are so many ways we can drink in his presence as we walk where all of creation is around us. Each season gives us a freshness of beauty. It is even interesting to observe how we walk differently on different surfaces, how we breathe more heavily as we walk up hills and inclines and feel the pull of certain muscles. How we walk more carefully on a wooded trail, more aggressive on solid terrain and in a plow like manner in shaky sand. These walks are a time for communication with the Creator. Cell phones and small electronic devices that keep us connected to the world must be left at home.

As I have spent time at the priory-monastery, frequently I would look out the front windows of the guest house and see a brother or sister walking, communing with God. Some utilize this time to pray the rosary therefore they are called "rosary walks." Just to observe them walking focused in prayer brings a depth of peace to the moment. One of the brothers following the peacefulness of the blessing of Compline bringing the day to a close, enjoys taking a brief walk around the beautiful natural grounds of the monastery. It is like a concluding Amen to the day of being in living prayer.

Some of us may find it helpful and satisfying to walk a labyrinth as we pray, meditate or ponder. Each step as we wind around the circles brings us to the center and a closer communion with Jesus.

Multitudes of people through the ages have committed themselves to walking a pilgrimage route or going to a site of special religious – spiritual significance. Among the most common would be the "Way of Saint James" or as referred to as the Route of Santiago de Compostela which concludes at the Cathedral of Santiago de Compostela in Galicia, Spain at the Shrine of Saint James the Great. Many pilgrims also visit the Cathedral in Chartres, France to view the magnificent stained glass windows, the tunic of the Virgin Mary which has been housed in the Cathedral since 876 AD. The stone floor still has its ancient labyrinth which was crafted in 1205 and was walked by monks as they contemplated. It is still used today by pilgrims as they choose to meditate. Another pilgrim destination is reached by sailing to the island of Iona in Scotland. This island received its renown by the coming of Saint Columba and twelve or thirteen of his followers who landed on this small island in 563

AD. He and his followers established an abbey. Today it is an ecumenical church and community working for peace, social justice and striving to walk humbly with God.

We are all walking a pilgrimage route, whether it is a formal trail or the way set before us. Each step, each mile, each path trod and mountain climbed in quest of a centering life is a prayer walk which is opening us more and more to the spirit of the living God.

Whether we choose a wooded path, a neighborhood street, a park, a mountain trail, a labyrinth or a full blown pilgrimage walk they all are prayer in communication with our Creator. Step by step we are being given his gifts of peace, joy, hope and the love that binds all gifts together.

FEED HIS SHEEP - SABBATH

"Love the Lord your God with all your heart and with all your soul and with all your mind and with all your strength. The second is this: 'Love your neighbor as yourself.' There is no other commandment greater than these."
Mark 12:30-31 (NIV)

"If we observe a true Sabbath we will feel a sense of wellness for our prayer will be one of rest that will invigorate the prayers of labor and action the other six days of the week."

After Jesus had been resurrected he appeared on the shore and invited his disciples to have a breakfast of fish and bread with him. As they were sharing this meal (a prayer breakfast – pause and think about this – how was this prayer?) Jesus asked, "Do you love me?" The reply was, "Yes!" He then told them to feed his sheep. Tend to and care for your neighbor and share my message.

There is a picture I appreciate of Saint Francis feeding a large variety of birds. Our neighbors come in many varieties as well. As we reach out to our neighbors through his great love, we are praying unceasing living prayer. This is expressing love for our Creator and because of his love dwelling in us we want to carry out his message by feeding his sheep with compassion, understanding and respect.

A Life of Living Prayer

Prayer is action, it is how we treat and serve our neighbor. Living prayer is "...to act justly, to love mercy and walk humbly with God." (Micah 6:8 NIV) This is the use of our gifts, beautiful gifts that God has blessed us with. Discerning our gifts may take some time, but through prayer, worship and the many channels and instruments he gives us we find our way and learn how to apply and share our gifts. However, we must have an open heart and mind to perceive and obtain a clearer vision as to the identification of these, our beautiful gifts. After we become aware of our gifts we need to find the path to use them that will glorify the Giver!

Our gifts need to be carefully and consciously pondered with the guidance of God. As this possibly slow discernment takes place we may experience unrest, pain, uncertainty, even loneliness and tears, but if our pondering and contemplation is sincere we shall echo the words of Psalm 126:5 (NIV paraphrase DAS), "Those who sow *(their thoughts and prayers) in tears will reap with songs of joy." When we truly find our gifts then we can share and receive his gift of heart dwelling joy.

God gave us the most beautiful gift possible, salvation and through that we reap the gifts to use – to carry out his prayer to feed his sheep.

We need to remember that gifts come in all sizes, but they are all of the same value. Our Giver looks upon each gift with the same eyes, just as he hears every prayer with the same ears. However, whatever the magnitude of our gift(s) they must be given to others with humility and sincerity or the gift is not from God's heart of love. Gifts from God only breathe and live through his generous love.

When we truly and thoughtfully work to carry out his vision and mission we need and must observe the Sabbath, the day of rest. After our Creator concluded his work of creation he rested. Do we really inter into Sabbath? We may attend worship, but is it just that? Do we carry on the spirit of the Sabbath throughout the day? The Sabbath should be a time of reflection on the past six days, a time of examination of our work. If we observe a true Sabbath we will feel a sense of wellness for our prayer will be one of rest that will invigorate the prayers of labor and action the other six days of the week.

In Exodus 20:8 (NIV) we are instructed to "Remember the Sabbath day by keeping it holy." This is achieved by fasting from the activity and labor of the other days. And just as prayer in the cell feeds our prayers of action out of the cell, so does disciplining ourselves to rest and breathe in his gift to all of us of peace and restoration.

SIMPLICTY AND FASTING

"...Foxes have their holes and birds of the air have their nests, but the Son of man has no place to lay his head."
Matthew 8:20 (NIV)

"For this life of simplicity we need to fast to remove the clutter, the rubbish, whatever keeps us from feeling his presence and being conscious of a life of prayer."

The familiar Shaker hymn, "Simple Gifts" which was written and composed by Elder Joseph Brackett has been shared through many generations. The Shakers did indeed live simply with bare bones living quarters, worked simply making practical furniture, baskets, clothes, growing and raising their own food. They believed this was giving to God. Religious orders live very frugally. Many live in simple cells, with usually a bed, chair, desk, kneeler and small closet for their few garments. This is to be as Christ like as possible and to live in simplicity so to have more time, energy and focus to give to their growing relationship with Jesus and their ministry of prayer. However, we are not Shakers or a religious in a monastic order. So how can we live simple lives?

It is "simple" but it is a difficult discipline. As we view each piece of furniture, knick knacks, collections and electronic equipment – what could we live without? Let us check our grocery shopping list, could we be more practical? How about our closets? Are the poles ready to collapse from the weight of our clothes? Do we spend money on many unnecessary and impractical items? We could go on and on and have a very lengthy list of what we think we need, but really don't. The bottom line is excessive or not, we need to be considerate of the needs of others. So often we think we are in a tight place, but we can always find someone who is in more need. But is this really what living simply is all about?

Ponder this, living simply is giving our time, talents (beautiful gifts), and treasures for the vision and mission of Jesus. Living simply means to put Jesus first and to not clutter our living with less important thoughts, deeds and material belongings. We need to take time to be with him, time to work with him, and time to examine what is done with and for him so as not to waste our time and energy. We also need to be alert to those around us who clutter our living. This is usually not intentional, but we need to be observant to this and graciously greet it through living prayer. He calls us to take up our cross and follow him. He calls us to have a life of living prayer. That is simplicity!

For this life of simplicity we need to fast and remove the clutter, the rubbish, whatever keeps us from feeling his presence and being conscious of a life of prayer. We all have our "stuff" that we need to examine to find if it is really all that important.

So frequently we will confide if I could only get away; go fishing, climb a mountain, walk on the beach, sit by a babbling brook, take a cruise I could relax and hopefully when I return I will be more slow paced and find the time I need to pray in and out of my cell. We know that his is really not the answer! We could travel the world even live in solitude for a time and return to reality and not be able to live a more simplistic life because it is not about what goes on around us it is what happens, lives within our heart of hearts.

Our calendars are black with ink, reminding us of this meeting, that appointment, but do we write in our time on the calendar for our quiet time in the cell to feed our work out of the cell?

Fasting is not only for a period of time, such as Lent, fasting is not just giving up food, it is relinquishing whatever takes away from centering on and serving Jesus the Christ. A word of caution, once the clutter in our lives is cleared away we must not replace it with some other clutter.

We cannot have true simplicity, without fasting. Simplicity is truly a gift from God, but we must work to receive it and use it.

Pray simply and live in simplicity for the fox has no room to clutter, the birds have small nests and our Lord had no place for it was all about living the will of his Father. From the humble manger in Bethlehem to the tomb of Joseph of Arimathea the path was one of simplicity.

PEOPLE WHO ARE BLESSINGS WHO ARE PRAYERS

"And I tell you that you are Peter, and on this rock, I will build my church..."
Matthew 16:18 (NIV)

"These special people are the instruments and channels that God works through to help us achieve our calling and discern our beautiful gifts and guide us in the use of them for his glory."

In the 1960s there was a movie that hit the screens and it is still being aired on television yearly, "The Sound of Music." I so remember seeing it at our local theater and thinking it was the greatest movie I had ever viewed. It still remains as one of my top five favorites. The scene that spoke to me with a very moving and inspiring message was when Maria, a young postulant who had been sent to be the governess of the Von Trapp children returned to the Abbey very confused about her life and was fearful she had fallen in love with Captain Von Trapp. For a young woman believing she had been called by God to be a nun this must have been extremely confusing for her and an anxious time of questioning. She had to listen for that "still small voice." The Abbess Mother called Maria into her

A Life of Living Prayer

study, listened to her, understood her confusion and prayerfully reminded her to seek and follow God's will. There is probably not a reader that does not know the conclusion of Maria's calling, but just in case someone missed this, she married Captain Von Trapp, World War II broke out and they fled to America and lived in Stowe, Vermont. The captain was Austrian and would not accept his post in the Third Reich, so he, Maria and the children, from his first marriage, escaped to freedom.

As each of us travel through life we find we have had and still have "Abbess Mothers" who inspire, guide and love us. If we journey back throughout our lives and even now as we live, breathe and move there are people who are true blessings given by God. They listen to us, observe us, guide us, feel and share our joys and sorrows and pray with and for us and that prayer is not only words but action as well. These special people are the instruments and channels that God works through to help us achieve our calling and discern our beautiful gifts and guide us in the use of them for his glory.

Right now let us take some time and journey back and come to the present and reflect on those who are truly prayers, blessings – "great" people in our life who have been our Mother Abbesses. These are the people we have been given as living prayers. Thanks be to God!

BREAKING THE BREAD AND DRINKING THE WINE

"This is my body, which is for you; do this in remembrance of me....this cup is the new covenant in my blood; do this, whenever you drink it, in remembrance of me."
I Corinthians 11:24-25 (NIV)

"Look, really look at that tiny piece of bread, it is not tiny. Look, really look at that tiny cup of wine it is not tiny."

There is nothing like a loaf of wholesome hardy grain bread. The aroma as it bakes and the texture and flavor as we partake of it truly enhances a meal. Families, friends and members of communities of faith gather to break bread and to enjoy their time and conversation together. However, how frequently do we pause and consider the message and importance of the bread?

When we receive our bread at communion do we really look at that little piece of bread and try to ponder all of its meaning for us as individuals and for the community of faith that we worship with and beyond to others who share in this remembrance, thanksgiving and prayer.

After his resurrection, Jesus walked from Jerusalem to Emmaus, about seven miles with two of his disciples, one named Cleopas, and as they talked they did not recognize him, but later realized that

A Life of Living Prayer

they had experienced a unique feeling as they traveled along the road. When they arrived at the village they invited Jesus in to break bread with them.

At that time Jesus took the bread, gave thanks and broke it and then began to share it with them. At that moment they recognized him. He left and they returned to Jerusalem and brought the news to the eleven disciples. We do not know why Jesus didn't stay to eat or maybe they didn't eat either for they were so filled with joyous news. Jesus had done his "job" and moved on to other followers to begin to prepare them for the future mission. The Emmaus Road travelers had been blessed and went back to the city to spread the news. What does this teach us? How is this praying continually? What does this teach us about people who come into our lives? Do we have the feeling as the Emmaus travelers did that there is something important and special happening?

This is not just about the breaking of bread at our tables or the table of remembrance, but about the drinking of the wine as well.

It is fascinating to watch a wine connoisseur testing their choice of wine. They roll it around in their glass, explore its "nose" and take a small sip and swish it around in their mouth, making all sorts of interesting expressions and negative or affirmative sounds. When we take the most precious wine of all do we pause to examine it and reflect on what it actually represents in our daily living? Do we ponder how this is prayer?

When we break the bread, we need to pause and examine it and reflect on what it actually represents in our daily living and ponder how this is prayer as well.

Take eat….take drink was his prayer as he sat around the table with his disciples. He himself prayed in the garden to not drink the cup of death for our salvation, but he received the strength, the great peace, the shalom to raise his cup on the cross for us and he prayed for us to raise up our cup, drink it and follow him. The body broken, the blood shed, do this in remembrance of me. Pause and ponder – do we recognize – do we pass it on?

The two travelers on the way to Emmaus recognized him and they went and told the bewildered, fearful, confused disciples, and they went and told and the story was passed on and on and now we have the bread and wine and now we have the joy of salvation, the victory of the cross to raise – the story to pass on. Do we consider the roots and contemplate the message, the responsibility and mission?

When we come to the table of remembrance we are indeed coming to the table where Jesus sat with his disciples and gave them the bread and wine and asked them to always do this in remembrance of him with thanksgiving. This was his prayer and every time we commune with him at the table we are carrying out his prayer and praying to him with hearts filled with gratitude.

Look, really look at that tiny piece of bread – it is not tiny. Look, really look at that tiny cup of wine – it is not tiny! Why is it not tiny? Because it is filled with his love and his prayer for us.

BREAKING BREAD AND DRINKING WINE

*Yahweh, always present in the bread
on the table of the tabernacle
Yahweh, always present in the manna as
his people wandered the wilderness
Yahweh, giver of our daily bread from the bounty
of the land and the richness of spiritual growth
Jesus, always present as the bread of life
Jesus, giver of bread to the multitudes as you
were present to give spiritual food
Jesus, always present in your broken body
of the bread received in remembrance
Yahweh, Eternal Father, Present Healer and Strength Giver,
Prince of Peace, Jesus the Christ, Lamb of God, Shepherd
of the Flock we give you our prayers of thanksgiving
The bread is broken and given, the cup is filled and shared
The presence of sorrow and joy
The presence of Love Divine
Holy Presence may we with contemplative
hearts eat and drink of your presence through
your sorrow which reveals complete joy
Divine Presence
Man of sorrows
Savior of joy*

Amen.

CONCLUSION OF PART ONE

"Pray continually"
I Thessalonians 5:17 (NIV)

*"How we pray is how we live and
how we live is how we pray"*

Let Us Ask

1. Do we really desire to deepen
our relationship with Jesus?
2. Do we feel called and drawn to a fuller,
more meaningful life of living prayer?
3. Are we willing to examine our life of living
prayer, our daily journey and our efforts to work
and carry out the vision and mission of Jesus?
4. Are we willing to listen to and with him and
patiently wait for his will his "still small voice?"
5. Are we willing to say, "no" to the busyness
of this world and all of the road blocks we
encounter and desire and spend time with him?
6. Are we willing to "clean house" and discipline
our body, mind and heart to know what is
important as Mary the sister of Martha did?
7. Are we willing to ponder our faith and the symbols
that draw us closer to the center of Jesus the Christ?
8. Are we willing to honestly and truthfully
honor the Sabbath, by resting and examining
the work, the seeds we planted and watered
during the other six days of the week?

9. Are we willing to be sensitive to the many channels and instruments that God gives us to support and guide us in our Christ centered journey?

10. Are we willing when we come together in worship to truly worship in spirit and in truth? Are we striving to really contemplate all we pray in worship whether it is what is traditionally labeled prayer, but also the hymns, call to worship, sermon and the experience of joining the hearts around the Table of Remembrance, Thanksgiving and Prayer?

11. Are we willing to consciously make the effort to be aware of his constant presence?

12. Are we ready to say not just with the mind, but heart as well, "Yes, Lord I am truly WITH you?"

A Life of Living Prayer

According to the Rule of Saint Benedict it is explained that we should prefer nothing to the Love of Christ. Whether we live in a religious order or out in the world we all have to discipline our living for Christ. Is it easy? No, but when his love calls us we become more focused and more graciously accept the challenge and it slowly becomes all prayer through his great and powerful love.

In the chapter concerning the praying of the hours, the conclusion was drawn that we who are not of a religious order can indeed be conscious of his presence from hour to hour even if we do not and can not visit a chapel to pray seven or more times a day. However, living in the guest house of a priory and monastery I have gained a much deeper appreciation of their calling and comprehend much more fully the meaning of Saint Benedict's philosophy of prayer and work is one if focused on God. That is what they do. They do pray in the chapel seven times a day singing the liturgy of the church in Gregorian chant. They also have time of solitude and silence and pray in fellowship with one another. They live very simply and they work several hours a day, each having and sometimes rotating responsibilities. Some garden and maintain the grounds and buildings, they care for the guest house, cook, clean, shop for groceries and other necessary items as well as take care of business responsibilities. This does not sound too much different from our living. Yes, they live in community and care for one another and I am sure there can be differences of opinion from time to time, but that does not get in the way of a commitment to live in prayer centered in

Jesus the Christ. Aren't we all "residents" in some kind of a community? This is a true example of how we pray is how we live and how we live is how we pray.

The sisters and the brothers pray as individuals, as community and this combination of prayer feeds into the strength of each other. As we center on Jesus, the living word in our individual prayers they will also feed into our communal prayers and our communal worship and these prayers will nourish our individual prayers and contemplations.

Prayer is more than a list, recited prayer, words of the mind, it is words and actions of the heart, it is prayer and work, it is what we feel through his presence. It is not a sentimental, gushy feeling, it is a strength, a joy and a peace that only comes through committed Christ centered prayer and that is what nurtures living prayer.

Jesus taught I am the living *Logos* - Word, I am the True Light, and I am the Living Water. If we consciously strive to show this in our living, we are his living example.

Living prayer has to be shared. When someone lives a life of living prayer we identify the burning oil in the lamp.

I was visiting a church one Sunday and the worship was truly meaningful, but when the pastor prayed it went beyond that. When the prayer concluded, I wanted more I did not want to move on, I simply wanted to stay with that feeling of Christ's living presence. As time went on I returned to that church

A Life of Living Prayer

several times and eventually joined. Why - because of the pastor's verbal prayer "The Prayers of the People," which he offers from the heart, but also because the way he prays is the way he lives and the way he lives is the way he prays. This is a genuine example of it is all prayer through his great love.

Go back, revisit the twelve questions and ask if I can become committed and disciplined to show forth the way I pray is the way I live and the way I live is the way I pray?

There was a 13 year girl who went to a Christian camp in up state New York, who was quite mature in her Christian journey and was very prone to go off by herself to commune with God. When she was at home she had a place apart in the woods next to her home. She would wander into the wooded grove and sit on a rock that was surrounded by velvety green moss. She particularly appreciated watching the sun cast shadows on it which changed the shades of green as she communed with the Creator. Well, when she was at camp this practice continued. Each evening before cabin devotions there was a half hour of free time. The teen-age girl found a large rock on the edge of the lake and sat on it and prayed as the ripples on the lake gently washed against one side of the rock. As she prayed the words to the hymn "Great Is Thy Faithfulness" came not only to her mind but her heart. A year before this girl's father had died and she was convinced that God had been faithful to her and her mother. There was emotion in that prayer but not sentimental or gushy, it was in thanksgiving and gratitude for the peace his faithfulness had provided. This girl is no longer 13, but she still sits on rocks and communes with God, and knows in the depth of her heart that prayer is a living organism when our lives are centered in and through the love of Jesus.

WRITTEN PRAYERS

Some pastors write the prayers they offer from the pulpit, which I strongly endorse for two reasons. Even the most eloquently praying pastors can offer rambling prayers from time to time and the congregation looses focus and the message and intent of the prayer. There could have been a blessing, healing words of caring and love there for us, but we missed it. Secondly, if they are written they can be shared as some pastors have their sermons available for the community of faith to read and ponder. Prayers do not usually stay in our memory. We hear them, even feel them, but once the Amen is said, we just move on to the remainder of the worship service. Maybe occasionally a thought or a few words will stay with us if it had touched us when we needed to hear those words because of situations in our life or someone we know. Most of the time we miss the impact of the entire prayer because we are not wired to retain or understand how we can apply these beautifully shared words to our life of living prayer.

Not only should prayers from the pulpit be pondered, but written prayers that are written for the purpose of being read. So often we will come across a book of prayers in a book store, purchase it, take it home and read the prayers as if it is a novel. We will read all 50 prayers and close the book and say that was nice and then move on. We even do this with quotes, never stopping to ponder the depth of those few words. We may play them over in our minds, but do we ponder them and get them secured in our muscle? The Spanish opera singer, Placido Domingo claimed that he rehearses his arias and other sections of each opera that he performs over and over so to get it into his muscle. We need to do that with prayers. Get out of the speed lane, read them slowly and ponder them asking how can I apply these words to my life of living prayer? As with so much of life we hurry, we drive over the speed limit in the far left lane. With written prayers we need to drive the winding country roads, experiencing the Creator's gifts around us.

Writing prayers is concentrated and ponderous work, it is quiet and listening work, it is loving and faithful sacred work. Prayers should be read in the same manner as they are written. There is an ancient pattern of reading scripture called Lectio Divina which being interpreted means divine reading. This is a traditional Benedictine practice of scripture reading, mediation, prayer and contemplation intended to foster a close communion with God's word. This is a wonderful historical practice that can be applied to written prayers as well. Read, take time to ponder and experience - feel what God is calling us to receive to guide us in a life of living prayer centered in his love.

GUIDE FOR READING, PONDERING AND APPLYING PRAYERS

1. Read the entire prayer slowly.
2. Re-read each line and/or phrase – ponder and summarize in a few sentences.
3. Contemplate and pray concerning how the message of this prayer can be applied to your living as you desire and strive to have a life of unceasing prayer.
4. Return and re-read the entire prayer. Are your thoughts and feelings different from the first time you read it? If so, how are they different and how did this happen?

More Thoughts on Reading, Pondering and Applying Prayers

1. You may want to only read one line and/or phrase at a time while you are in your cell, place apart and take a long period of time to have his message in this particular line and/or phrase work into your muscle.
2. When you have completed the prayer leave it for a while and then return. Examine how it has guided your life of prayer and discern if you are still having the same thoughts as when you began this prayer.

PART TWO
WRITTEN PRAYERS
By Dawn A. Sweet
The following prayers were inspired
by sermons and/or prayers given
By Thomas R. McKibbens
At the First Baptist Church, Worcester, Massachusetts
And
The First Baptist Meeting House (Church)
of America, Providence, Rhode Island

"On Eagles Wings"

"Silence, Sheer Silence"

"Bread and Blessing"

"Doors and Gates"

"The Eternal Message"

"Donkey Detail"

"Grace from the Cross"

"Rivers and Tributaries"

"Be Blessed"

"Peace, Deep Peace"

"Great – Everlasting Faithfulness"

"Tears, Faith, Joy and Peace"

WRITTEN PRAYERS – CONTINUED
By Dawn A. Sweet

"Nothing, No Nothing"

"Father, Forgive"

"Pray"

"The Day I Stood"

"His Light, Our Light"

"Blessings of Each Day"

"Selah"

"A Gift of Mercy"

"A Meal of Prayer"

"Ponder"

"But for you who revere my name, the son of righteousness will rise with healing in its wings. And you will go out and leap like calves released from the stall."
Malachi 4:2 (NIV)

ON EAGLES WINGS

God of great strength
Wings that spread
Wings that embrace
Wings of great heights
Wings that sweep the earth
Wings that encourage us to be a people of grace
A people of acceptance
A people of faith
A people of courage
A people of fortitude
A people of endurance
A people of justice
A people of shalom
A people of harmony
A people of forgiveness
A people of trust
A people of pardon
A people of compassion
A people of mercy
A people of sensitivity
A people of love
A people of devotion
A people of a great gift

Dawn A. Sweet

> *May we be lifted to new horizons*
> *Granted with fogless vision and clearer views*
> *With wings that spread*
> *With wings that embrace*
> *With wings of great heights*
> *With wings that sweep the earth*
> *With wings that encourage us to be a people of grace*
> *Amen.*

A Life of Living Prayer

"Be still and know that I am God..."
Psalm 46:10 (NIV)
"After the earthquake came a fire, but the Lord was not in the fire. And after the fire came a gentle whisper."
I Kings 19:12 (NIV)

SILENCE, SHEER SILENCE

Beloved Voice of Silence
We hear
The voices of evil temptation
The voices of danger
The voices of drought
The voices of frustration
The voice of misunderstanding
The voices of anger
The voices of doubt
The voices of betrayal
The voices of neediness
The voices of darkness
The voices of pain
The voices of unbearable noise
They haunt us, perplex us, annoy us
And draw us away from that "still small voice."
The voice of good encouragement
The voice of safety
The voice of generous watering
The voice of comfort
The voice of understanding
The voice of forgiveness

Dawn A. Sweet

The voice of knowing
The voice of acceptance
The voice of assurance
The voice of relief
The voice of welcome silence
This voice sooths us, assures us, guides us
This is God coming gently, peacefully through
The back door of our heart
Silence, silence, silence – sheer silence
Amen.

"...taking the five loaves and the two fish and looking up to heaven, he gave thanks and broke the loaves. Then he gave them to the disciples, and the disciples gave them to the people. They all ate and were satisfied..."
Matthew 14:19-20 (NIV)

"Jesus declared, 'I am the bread of life...'"
John 6:35 (NIV)

BREAD – BLESSINGS

Giver of bread
Bounty of grain
In the wilderness
Before the multitudes
On tables of feasting and sharing
On tables of thanksgiving and gratitude
Giver of bread
Bounty of grain
Receiving through prayer
Receiving through worship
Receiving through scripture
Receiving through fellowship
Receiving through divine goodness and love
Giver of bread
Bounty of grain
The blessing and breaking of bread
before the Emmaus disciples
Eating of bread in the early morning on
the shore – feeding his sheep

Dawn A. Sweet

Praying for daily bread for body, mind and soul
The tiny piece of bread as the center of
our worship and remembrance
The bread of life that "nourishes us to the depths of our soul"
Giver of bread
Bounty of grain
God's blessing
Amen.

*"Here I am! I stand at the door and knock. If
anyone hears my voice and opens the door, I will
come in and eat with him, and he with me."
Revelation 3:20 (NIV)*

*"Enter through the narrow gate…but small is the
gate and narrow the road that leads to life…"
Matthew 7:13-14 (NIV)*

DOORS AND GATES

*We are moved by his pulse to place our hand on the knob
To pull the door open
To come inside
To worship with our neighbors
To share fellowship one with another
To open the door of our heart
To feel his divine presence and love
To eat of his life giving nourishment
We sometimes pause at the door or gate
A little nervous to accept the gifts inside
Not quite open to walk his road of covenant and commitment
Not quite willing for a fresh watering of
the dry areas within our hearts
Not quite sure about praying with open hands, soul and mind
Not quite trusting in his will for our lives
Not quite secure and struggling with doubt
But still his pulse places our hand on the knob and we enter
To dine with him receiving his life giving nourishment
That "still small voice" is an intense – passionate pulse
Thanks Be to God!
Amen.*

> "The days are coming, says the Lord, when I will make a new covenant…I will put my law within them, and I will write it on their hearts and I will be their God, and they shall be my people."
> Jeremiah 31:31,33 (NRSV)

THE ETERNAL MESSAGE

Eternal Yahweh you taught:
Keep the message
Within your heart
In your muscle
Alive for your neighbor to witness
Interesting for your children to learn
Visible in your coming and going
Retain the brightness in your lamp

Eternal Yahweh you gave the message
The message has lived on through
Prophets
Disciples
Communities of faith
Prayer
Worship
Fellowship
Vision
Eternal Yahweh you required us to worship you
The message was to worship from the heart
Not through fad
Not through business

Not through nostalgia
Not through the pressures of the time
Not through change for change sake
Not through piety
Eternal Yahweh you love us to write
your message on our hearts
Eternal Yahweh may we love you enough
to water and feed our hearts
No matter the cultural climate or the weather
Eternal Yahweh we are your people
We realize the tides rise and fall, but your message remains
For it is ETERNAL!
Amen.

"...Go to the village ahead of you, and just as you enter it, you will find a colt tied there, which no one has ridden. Untie it and bring it here."

Mark 11:2 (NIV)

DONKEY DETAIL

For all who strive to serve the Christ
It is loyalty
It is commitment
It is patience
It is energy
It is courage
It is strength
It is love

It is listening to repetitious stories
It is being patient with needy souls
It is striving to heal a negative spirit
It is reaching out to unpleasant situations
It is breaking bread with one who is "hungry"
It is giving love when all around are bitter and deceptive
It is being silent when words can do harm

We received the message, the duty, the donkey detail
We have all stood deep in the mire for Jesus
But that mire is the fragrance of expensive perfume
Amen.

"Jesus said, 'forgive them…'"
Luke 23:34 (NIV)

GRACE, FROM THE CROSS

On that day
God the Father prayed
Jesus the Son prayed
Humankind, your children, prayed

Grace was there bleeding painfully –
sorrowfully from the cross
Forgiveness was offered with and without our petition
Compassion was shared and taught
for us to care for one another
An abandonment and loneliness pierced his broken heart
A parching thirst was unable to be quenched
He drank his cup empty
His spirit was given up for us

Was our prayer full of self?
Was our prayer fueled with anger?
Was our prayer laden with misunderstanding?
Was our prayer riddled with guilt?
Was our prayer blinded by sin?
Was our prayer encompassed with doubt?
Was our prayer carved out of honesty?

Was our prayer one of gratitude?
Was our prayer one of compassion?

Was our prayer one of pain within and without?
Was our prayer open and accepting?
Was our prayer one of sincerity?
Was our prayer one of humility?
Was our prayer one of love?

At the foot of the cross there was darkness
At the foot of the cross there was light
At the foot of the cross there was GRACE!

GOD OF GRACE – THANK YOU!
Amen.

A Life of Living Prayer

"Fruit trees of all kinds will grow on both banks of the river. Their leaves will not wither, nor will their fruit fall. Every month they will bear, because the Water from the Sanctuary flows from (through) them. Their fruit will serve for food and their leaves for healing."
Ezekiel 47:12 (NIV)

RIVERS AND TRUBUTARIES

Dear Creator, for the river that nourishes the
land and the fruit we are grateful
For the Living Water that nourishes our souls we are grateful
For the blessed water of our baptism we are grateful
For the river we follow as your waterway
of ministry we are grateful

Divine Guide you have given us the love to bear fruit
You have guided us to sometimes walk in shallow water
You have guided us to sometimes walk in deep water
You have guided us to sometimes leave the river
and nourish those along the tributaries

Dear Enlightener, envision us to see the fruit that has
grown on both sides of the river and along the tributaries
Envision us to see how this fruit will mature (telios –
Greek) as it drinks the Living Water of agape
Envision us to see your humble spirit at work
Envision us to see and feel the great healing
that flows from the Living Water

In the spirit of the Creator
Amen.

Dawn A. Sweet

"The Lord bless you and keep you; the Lord make his face to shine upon you and be gracious to you; the Lord lift his countenance upon you and give you peace."
Numbers 6:24-26 (NIV & NRSV)

BE BLESSED

Blessed by God and only God
His blessings are there through all of life
The calm waters and the roaring seas
The sun drenched days and the wet soggy hours
The moments of laughter and the occasions of tears
The fullness of being together and the
emptiness of being apart
The exciting days of festival and the solemn days of mourning
Blessed by God and only God

Blessed by God and only God
His blessings are tried and true
We are swaddled in his grace
We are covered in his compassion
We are bundled in his mercy
We are shrouded in his presence
We are embraced in his love
Blessed by God and only God

Blessed by God and only God
His blessings come through the light of creation
His light came out of pure darkness
He warms us with the sun by day

He guides us with the stars by night
He fills our hearts with light
He gives us oil in our lamps so to shine through his light
Blessed by God and only God

Blessed by God and only God
His blessings are the bearers of peace
His peace is deep
His peace is planted within the furrows of our soul
His peace penetrates through his light, the glow of his face
His peace is all encompassing
His peace, his shalom, is the wholeness that we need for living
Blessed by God and only God
Amen.

*"Peace I leave with you; my peace I give to you.
I do not give as the world gives. Do not let you
hearts be troubled and do not be afraid."*
John 14:27 (NIV)

PEACE, DEEP PEACE

*Savior of peace, too deep to describe
You gave it to your disciples
You give it to us today
Do we recognize it when it gently fills and covers us?
Is it so deep we not only pray with words
of gratitude, but with tears?*

*You taught peace when you were feeling
*"the dark night of the soul"
When you were about to be betrayed, denied,
judged, abandoned and crucified
You Prince of Peace, was shrouded with the
peace, deep peace at the darkest of hours
As you prayed with words and tears, you fully drank
your cup as your soul was drenched with peace*

*We all have our dark nights, our Gethsemane;
we all have our cup to drink
When that blessing of peace enters – even all around
us is still dark our soul knows all is well
Can we share this gift, the deep gift of peace?*

A Life of Living Prayer

*We can speak about inner peace, but thank you Dear
Giver for giving it as a personal - individual silence when
we are journeying through "the dark night of the soul."
It is peace, deep peace too deep for words
It is received in silence and kept in silence*

*It was night, you received that deep peace
Did you tell your disciples? No, you simply said,
"the hour is near" and was taken off into the dark
of night, filled with Deep Divine Peace!
Savior – Teacher, thank you for your example and deep
gift of peace that comes through the darkness of night
Amen.*

** Title of a poem by the 16th century Spanish
Mystic known as:"Saint John of the Cross."
Written in 1578 or 1579 and full treatise between 1584-85.*

Dawn A. Sweet

> *"The steadfast love of the Lord never ceases,
> his mercies never come to an end: They are new
> every morning; great is Thy faithfulness."*
> *Lamentations 3:22-23 (RSV)*

GREAT – EVERLASTING FAITHFULNESS

When the valley is cloudy, he is faithful
When the valley is sunny, he is faithful

When the words are painful, he is faithful
When the words are pleasant, he is faithful

When the path is steep, he is faithful
When the path is level, he is faithful

When the heart is pierced, he is faithful
When the heart is singing, he is faithful

When the frustrations of life are at high tide, he is faithful
When the frustrations of life are at low tide, he is faithful

When the blindness of injustice is reaching out, he is faithful
*When the sight of justice replaces the
blindness of injustice, he is faithful*

When the understanding of all around is weak, he is faithful
*When the understanding of all around
is strengthened, he is faithful*

When the tears of sorrow roll, he is faithful
When the tears of joy roll, he is faithful

Blessed assurance — for great and
everlasting is his faithfulness
Promise — everything there is a season — for
everything there is his blessing of
Faithfulness through his great love
Amen.

> "By the rivers of Babylon we sat and wept when we
> remembered Zion. There on the poplars we hung our harps for
> there our captors asked us for songs, our tormentors demanded
> songs of joy they said 'Sing us one of the songs of Zion.'"
> Psalm 137:1-2 (NIV)
>
> "You will go out with joy and be led forth in peace…"
> Isaiah 55:12 (NIV)

TEARS, FAITH, JOY AND PEACE

God of Zion, God of the beloved Jerusalem
we fall upon our knees and weep
Our music of joy offered for your ears has ceased
Our pain is great
Our grief is deep
Our understanding is weak
Where is the joy we once knew?
Where are the bright sun, moon and
stars shinning over our land?
Where are the men who pray in the Temple?
Where are the women who keep the warm hearth burning?
Where are the children who happily
prattle and play in the by-ways?
Where are those days when the land was
springing up with milk and honey?
Yahweh, God of Abraham, Isaac and Jacob, may we remember
you, may we once again sing songs of joy for your ears

God of all nations, God of the many villages of
the world we fall upon our knees and weep

Our music of joy offered for your ears has ceased
Our pain is great
Our grief is deep
Our understanding is weak
Where is the joy we once knew?
Where are the bright sun, moon and
stars shinning over our land?
Where are all those who pray in the houses of worship?
Where are all those who give maternal nurturing?
Where are the children who happily giggle
and walk to school without fear?
Where are those days when the land was
springing up with milk and honey?
God of all Lands may we remember you, may we
once again sing our songs of joy for your ears

God of communities of faith, God of our pilgrim
fathers we fall upon our knees and weep
Our music of joy offered for your ears has ceased
Our pain is great
Our grief is deep
Our understanding is weak
Where is the joy we once knew?
Where are the bright sun, moon and stars
over our communities of faith?
Where are all of those who faithfully pray
within your earthly kingdom?
Where are the carefully and lovingly taught lessons
of "love your neighbor" within the home?

*Where are the children that dance for joy
around the Sunday school table?
Where are those days when the communities of
faith were springing up with milk and honey?
God of our foundation may we remember you, may
we once again sing our song of joy for your ears.*

*God of our personal soul, God of our private
journey we fall upon our knees and weep
Our music of joy offered for your ears has ceased
Our pain is great
Our grief is deep
Our understanding is weak
Where is the joy we once knew?
Where are the bright sun, moon and
stars shinning within our lives?
Where are we who faithfully pray seeking your guidance?
Where in the home are we struggling with
the many vicissitudes of life?
Where are the children, are they being
swayed by negative forces?
Where are those days when our lives were
springing up with milk and honey?
God of healing, may we remember you, may we
once again sing our songs of joy for your ears*

*God of yesterday, God of today and tomorrow we
fall upon our knees and relinquish our resentment,
despair, feelings of rejection, bitterness and struggle
May our music be offered not only from our lips, but our heart*

May our comfort be great
May our peace be deep
May our understanding be strengthened
May our joy be restored
May we see the bright sun, moon and
stars shinning in our life
At home, may we not be "heavy laden" with
frustration and a multitude of disappointments
May our children learn of true faith so not to
succumb to the weakness of the world
May we recognize we do indeed have milk and honey
springing up around us through your gracious love and mercy

God of eternity, may we worship, offer our music of joy for
your ears and go out with that same joy and not only return
with peace, but live in and around the Great Shalom!
Amen.

Dawn A. Sweet

"Neither height nor depth, or anything else in all creation, will be able to separate us from the love of God that is in Christ Jesus our Lord."

Romans 8:39 (NIV)

NOTHING, NO NOTHING

Dear God of love, understanding and compassion
We do acknowledge that there is indeed a balm in Gilead
"peace I leave with you, my peace I give unto you,"
Yes, there is Shalom!
We hear and feel words of misunderstanding
Yes, there is Shalom!
We hear and feel the words of impatience
Yes, there is Shalom!
We hear and feel the words of this world,
even in his communities of faith
Yes, there is Shalom!
We know some thoughts and deeds are not
focused in the mission of the church
Yes, there is Shalom!
We acknowledge that there are those who do not
Clearly see the Vision of Jesus the Christ
Yes, there is Shalom!
We sense the urge that some want change
even if it is not necessary
Yes, there is Shalom!
We feel the energy of control through
the avenues of financial power
Yes, there is Shalom!

*We are saddened by the lack of respect for
experience, knowledge and wisdom
Yes, there is Shalom!
We feel there are some whose worship is shallow
due to preoccupation with the business at hand
Yes, there is Shalom!
We through all of this know that NOTHING, NO
NOTHING can separate us from the love, understanding
and compassion of our ever faithful God!
Amen and Shalom.*

> *"…Father forgive them, for they do not*
> *know what they are doing…"*
> *Luke 23:34 (NIV)*

FATHER FORGIVE

Father, forgive me when I do not listen
Father, forgive me when I do not pray
Father, forgive me when I do not take time for silence
Father, forgive me when I do not obey
Father, forgive me when I do not exhibit patience
Father, forgive me when I do not extend compassion
Father, forgive me when my motives are wrong
Father, forgive me when I do not love

Father, give me open ears to hear
Father, give me a desire to pray
Father, give me a yearning for silence
Father, give me an obedient spirit
Father, give me the fortitude for patience
Father, give me the depth of compassion
Father, give me the gift of sensitivity
Father, give me the honesty for your motives
Father, give me the urgency of love

Father, enrich me with your wisdom
Father, open me to forgive as you forgive
Father, inspire me to grow into a deeper relationship with you
Father, decrease my predisposition to be judgmental
Father, guide me to intercede for others

Father, humble me to seek and follow your will
Father, remove the barriers I feel between us and one another
Father, help my unbelief
Amen.

Dawn A. Sweet

"When one serves others through the love of God, they are like the light of morning at sunrise on a cloudless morning, like the brightness after rain that brings grass from the earth."
II Samuel 23:3-4 (NIV and Paraphrase by DAS)

PRAY

God of healing – God of love
God of light - God of rebirth

When the mountain is too steep and treacherous, pray
When the water is too deep and turbulent, pray
When the wind is gusty and cold, pray
When the rain is heavy and chilling, pray
When the lightening streaks and flashes, pray
When the thunder rumbles and shakes, pray
When the rose is thorny and wilting, pray
When the bread is old and stale, pray
When the wine is bitter and flavorless, pray

When humility is waning or absent, pray
When respect is waning or absent, pray
When understanding is waning or absent, pray
When sensitivity is waning or absent, pray
When compassion is waning or absent, pray
When wisdom is waning or absent, pray
When shalom is waning or absent, pray
When gratitude is waning or absent, pray
When healing is waning or absent, pray
When love is waning or absent, pray

When the mountain becomes a hill with
smoother terrain, someone prayed
When the water is shallow and calm, someone prayed

A Life of Living Prayer

*When the wind is tranquil and still, someone prayed
When the rain is over and the sun appears, someone prayed
When the lightening fades and ceases, someone prayed
When the thunder quiets and stops, someone prayed
When the rose is blooming and fragrant, someone prayed
When the bread is fresh and savory, someone prayed
When the wine is pleasant and flavorful, someone prayed
When life is bright and fulfilling, someone prayed*

*When humility visits and returns, someone prayed
When respect visits and returns, someone prayed
When understanding visits and returns, someone prayed
When sensitivity visits and returns, someone prayed
When compassion visits and returns, someone prayed
When wisdom visits and returns, someone prayed
When shalom visits and returns, someone prayed
When gratitude visits and returns, someone prayed
When healing visits and returns, someone prayed
When love visits and returns, someone prayed*

*God of healing – God of love
God of light – God of rebirth*

*This we pray with gratitude in the spirit of your Divine Love.
Amen.*

Dawn A. Sweet

> *"…all of you clothe yourselves with humility…"*
> *I Peter 5:5 (NIV)*

THE DAY I STOOD

Dear Savior

The day I stood at the foot of the cross I was uncertain
Help my unbelief

The day I stood at the foot of the cross I was anxious
Give me peace

The day I stood at the foot of the cross I was weak
Grant me strength

The day I stood at the foot of the cross my heart was empty
Fill it with your love

The day I stood at the foot of the cross I was full of self
Grow me into humility

The day I stood at the foot of the cross I was closed
Open me to your guidance

The day I stood at the foot of the cross I was in darkness
Give me your light

The day I stood at the foot of the cross I was burdened
Place your yoke upon me

A Life of Living Prayer

The day I stood at the foot of the cross
I was a wandering lamb
Focus me into your mission

The day I stood at the foot of the cross I
was a garden that needed weeding
Remove the weeds and help me blossom

The day I stood at the foot of the cross I heard you pray
Please let me feel you pray
Amen.

Dawn A. Sweet

> *"You are the light of the world. A city*
> *on a hill cannot be hidden."*
> *Matthew 5:14 (NIV)*

HIS LIGHT, OUR LIGHT

Advent the light of hope, peace, joy and love
Do I receive that light?
Do I cultivate that light?
Do I freely offer that light through my living?

Christmas the light of humanity through the divine
Do I receive that light?
Do I cultivate that light?
Do I freely offer that light through my living?

Ordinary time the light of growth
Do I receive that light?
Do I cultivate that light?
Do I freely offer that light through my living?

Lent the light of repentance and examination
Do I receive that light?
Do I cultivate that light?
Do I freely offer that light through my living?

Palm Sunday the light of receiving him as Lord
Do I receive that light?
Do I cultivate that light?
Do I freely offer that light through my living?

The Passover – The Lord's Supper the light of remembrance
Do I receive that light?
Do I cultivate that light?
Do I freely offer that light through my living?

The prayer in the garden the light of surrender
Do I receive that light?
Do I cultivate that light?
Do I freely offer that light through my living?

The judgment hall the light of profession
Do I receive that light?
Do I cultivate that light?
Do I freely offer that light through my living?

The crucifixion the light of salvation
Do I receive that light?
Do I cultivate that light?
Do I freely offer that light through my living?

The resurrection the light of assurance
Do I receive that light?
Do I cultivate that light?
Do I freely offer that light through my living?

The message, "feed my sheep" the light of his mission
Do I receive that light?
Do I cultivate that light?
Do I freely offer that light through my living?

Dawn A. Sweet

The day of Pentecost the light of energy
Do I receive that light?
Do I cultivate that light?
Do I freely offer that light through my living?

Ordinary time the light of growth
Do I receive that light?
Do I cultivate that light?
Do I freely offer that light through my living?

Savior, Shepherd, Teacher, Strength, Greatest Light
You commissioned
You promised
You fulfilled
Inspire, enlighten me to stay in that commission and promise
Pour the oil freely into my lamp so I may
be a messenger of fulfillment.
Amen.

A Life of Living Prayer

"I will make a covenant of peace with them....I will send down showers in season; there will be showers of blessings."
Ezekiel 34: 25-26 (NIV)

BLESSINGS OF EACH DAY

Creator of your time, may we slow to it
Create in us the concentration of patience

Open us to examine our daily living in each season of life
Free us from selfish egotism to accept your will

In surrender to your will bring realization
of your true blessings
Through a faithful walk, may the dew upon
our feet come as a cool blessing

Each day you pour rain drops of blessings into our living
Some days you drench us with heavy rain
showers of abundant blessings

In tune our senses to sense the quick coming drops of blessings
Search our souls so to prepare us for the
greater showers of blessings

As the dew refreshes the splendid grass
As the sprinkles of water dampens the soil
As the showers of rain feeds the roots of vegetation
May the dew of blessings alert us
May the sprinkles of water refresh us

Dawn A. Sweet

May the showers of rain bring an open drenching to our soul

Creator of the old covenant and the new covenant
Slow us to your time

Create in us the concentration of patience
So that through the dew, sprinkles and showers
we will know and feel your blessings.

Amen.

*"Finally, brothers, whatever is true, whatever
is noble, whatever is right, whatever is
pure, whatever is lovely, whatever is admirable – if anything
is excellent or praiseworthy – think about such things."
Philippians 4:8 (NIV)*

*"SELAH"
(Pause and think about it, ponder it.)*

*Jesus Christ, our teacher, our guide,
our inspiration, our example
May we ponder what you taught through
words, silence and action
May we ponder our journey as you guide us
May we ponder our receiving of your many gifts and
blessings that inspire us to live and share your truth
May we ponder your divine and human example so
to reach out through your great and infinite love*

*May we ponder your work as a carpenter, one who builds
May we ponder your baptism taking
on the mission of your Father
May we ponder your time in the wilderness
struggling with the power of temptation
May we ponder your message through your
parables claiming your message for living
May we ponder your miracles and see beyond the
physical healing into the spiritual recovery
May we ponder the times you needed to be
alone and commune with your Father*

*May we ponder and truly give praise and adoration
to you as King of Kings and Lord of Lords
May we ponder your prayer of remembrance to eat the bread
and drink the cup holding forth the great thanksgiving
May we ponder your prayer of tears as you
fully surrendered in the garden
May we ponder your strength and patience
as you were judged throughout the night of
torment, but also throughout your ministry
May we ponder your prayers from the cross
for you were still giving and teaching
May we ponder your fulfillment of your Father's
plan as we walk our "Emmaus Road"*

*May we ponder our calling, our journey, our ministry and
examine it with openness so to show forth your teachings,
your guidance, your inspiration and your example.*

Amen.

A Life of Living Prayer

"…the Lord is full of compassion and mercy."
James 5:11(NIV)

A GIFT OF MERCY

Written for the Sisters of Saint Scholoastica
Priory, Petersham, Massachusetts
in appreciation of their welcoming spirit and free giving love.

God, come to my assistance
Lord, make haste to help me
In your presence Lord, show me my neighbor
Sight my vision so to see you in them
Kyrie eleison. Christe eleison. Kyrie eleison.

God, come to my assistance
Lord, make haste to help me
In your presence Lord, help me to truly examine myself
Open me so I may serve you with an open selfless heart
Kyrie eleison. Christe eleison. Kyrie eleison.

God, come to my assistance
Lord, make haste to help me
In your presence Lord, create a soul filling peace
Over flow me with this peace so others will
observe the depth of your shalom
Kyrie eleison. Christe eleison. Kyrie elesion.

God, come to my assistance
Lord, make haste to help me
In your presence Lord, grant me your forgiveness
Incline me to be forgiving of others
Kyrie eleison. Christe eleison. Kyrie eleison.

God, come to my assistance

Dawn A. Sweet

> *Lord, make haste to help me*
> *In your presence Lord, fill me with your everlasting light*
> *Strengthen me to climb the hill and be a*
> *bright beacon showing your glory*
> *Kyrie eleison. Christe eleison. Kyrie eleison.*
>
> *God, come to my assistance*
> *Lord, make haste to help me*
> *In your presence Lord, quicken my step*
> *Energize me to run the race before me*
> *always carrying your torch*
> *Kyrie eleison. Christe elesion. Kyrie eleison.*
>
> *God, come to my assistance*
> *Lord, make haste to help me*
> *In your presence Lord, feed me so to be a*
> *true branch of your living vine*
> *Ripen and sweeten your fruit so others will taste and see*
> *Kyrie eleison. Christe eleison. Kyrie eleison.*
>
> *God, come to my assistance*
> *Lord, make haste to help me*
> *In your presence Lord, help me to surrender to your great love*
> *Enlarge my heart to pulsate your love*
> *through a life of living prayer*
> *Kyrie eleison. Christe eleison. Christe eleison.*
> *In the spirit of Christ.*
> *Amen.*

"Jesus said to them,' Come and have breakfast..."'
John 21:12 (NIV)

"A MEAL OF PRAYER"

God, the giver of physical and spiritual food,
you join us together in your faithful love
When we come together to share your food may
our thoughts be centered in your presence
Guide our conversation to be words of respect
Guide our conversation to be words of understanding
Guide our conversation to be words of honest friendship
Guide our conversation to be words of agape

As we sit at the table being nourished by the bounty of the
earth, may we be nourished by the bounty of your presence
May we realize that we are giving to each other
through the fellowship of the "Tie that Binds"
As we break the bread and savor our generous plate of food
may we be thankful and joyous in this time of gathering
As we converse about life may we see one
another as a channel of your love
As the meal progresses may we not only receive
physical energy, but energy for the soul
As the coffee and dessert are enjoyed may we feel
the prayer that began as we came to the table,
shared food for the body and food for the soul
As we leave to go our separate ways may the "Amen"
continue to echo in the chambers of our heart

For you, God the giver of physical and spiritual food who
brought us together we give thanks for your faithful love
Amen.

Dawn A. Sweet

"Be still and know that I am God…"
Psalm 46:10 (NIV)

PONDER

*God of Abraham, Isaac and Jacob you sent
him in humility with eyes of love
God of Simeon, you sent a sign of hope
with eyes of peace – shalom
God of humanity, you sent him to take on our
transgressions with eyes of mission
God of prophesy and learning, you sent him
as a teacher with eyes of clarity
God of sacrifice, you sent him to pay the
price for us with eyes of weeping
God of victory, you sent him to be
resurrected with eyes of assurance
Ponder!*

*God who sent him with a vision, a mission -
has also given us a vision and a mission
God who gave him gifts to use and share,
also gives us gifts to use and share
God who gave him people to teach also
gives us those who want to learn
God who gave him souls to heal through love, also
gives us souls that need healing through love
God who gave him great light, also gives us oil in our lamps*

God who gave him with complete joy, also
gives us fuller joy as we feed his sheep
Ponder!

God of creation, the creator of the sights and
sounds around us, may we see, may we listen
God of unity, the unifier of our communities
of faith, may we see, may we listen
God of our journey, the guide of each
step, may we see, may we listen
God of our testimony, the author of our
witness, may we see, may we listen
God of our song, the composer of each
Note, may we see, may we listen
God of our call, the strength of fulfillment,
may we see, may we listen
Ponder!

God you have called throughout the ages
through sights and sounds all around us
God you have called us through printed word
God you have called us through your
channels and instruments
God you have called us through prayer
God you have called us in places and
circumstances that we cannot fathom
God you have called us through that "still small voice"
Ponder!

Dawn A. Sweet

> *God you have called us to feed your sheep*
> *God you have called us to open and to grow through your grace*
> *God you have called us to remembrance*
> *God you have called us to see you in our neighbors*
> *God you have called us to faithfully feel your presence*
> *God you have called us to follow in your foot prints of love*
> *Ponder!*

> *God, may we know your humility*
> *God, may we know your peace – shalom*
> *God, may we live your message*
> *God, may we feed your sheep*
> *God, may we have the oil in our lamps that keeps us burning*
> *God, may we eat the bread and drink the wine of*
> *your true love with more than remembrance*
> *Ponder!*

> *In the spirit of our living Christ. Amen and Amen!*

EPILOGUE

In the Preface you read about the most common ways we as children learned to pray and ways we continued to pray into our adult lives. As you have studied and pondered the various paths of prayer and the composed prayers in this written guide I hope you have begun to analyze where you are in the journey of unceasing prayer and how you can move on and experience a fuller life of living prayer.

In Deuteronomy 6:6-8 (NIV paraphrase DAS) we are instructed that the commandments (lessons) that are given and taught to us each day are to be on our hearts, in our muscle. We are to impress them upon our children, our neighbors. Talk about them when we sit at home with family and friends and when we walk along the road with our traveling partner, when we lie down and when we get up willing to share the message at all times. Tie them as symbols on our head and bind them on our foreheads, be an example of his joy, peace, light and love. Write them upon the doorframes of our houses and on our gates. Always extend a prayerful welcoming spirit. This is continuous prayer, it is living prayer.

As we take time in our special place(s) our place apart with him may we quiet ourselves to his "still small voice." If we first ponder his lessons and his message and then go into the world, walk the roads and avenues showing forth his joy, peace, light and love we then become examples of living prayer.

Our prayers are not just words, lists of people and situations, they are words of examination as well. As mentioned earlier without examination we are treading water, not being honest about our praying through words, silence and action. Our prayers need to speak and show forth thanksgiving as well as adoration and praise.

As I write this I can gaze out onto the back yard of the guest house of the Saint Scholastica Priory and Saint Mary's Monastery and be reminded that the Creator is there through the beautiful wild flowers, the very green of the foliage and ferns that grow wildly, unattended by man. There are honey bees gathering nectar from the clover and butterflies being attracted to the purple and pink gifts of nature. As I am reflecting, I hear the lock in the front door being opened. I glanced up and saw Monica standing there with morning coffee and a blueberry muffin to share. She resides approximately thirty minutes away and frequently comes to spend a day or an over night so to simply be, listen, pray, read and enjoy fellowship. Later Brother Isidore, the guest house master, arrived with a new guest and after he got the new comer settled in the Brother and I shared prayerful conversation which we did several times during my time at the guest house. Through all of this; nature of the out-of-doors, sharing a muffin with a new friend and having dialogue with the Brother is knowing and feeling his presence, feeling the prayer that was being shared.

There are symbols of our faith all around us and as we see them we are reminded of his presence. In our church buildings we have a numerous variety of symbols, in our homes, maybe where we work, but symbols of God's unceasing love are also seen as we look at our neighbor and all of God's creation. With all of these in our field of vision, we are constantly praying, hour by hour, moment by moment.

Whether we follow a short path, wander around a labyrinth, or walk a pilgrimage route it is a journey with him. It is time to commune with him so to be able to work with him in a more understanding and compassionate way. Even if we are not taking a "prayer walk" our daily walking should be in his footsteps, praying through the ebb and flow of the day.

Each week there is a full Sabbath, but each day we can pause and take the time for an abbreviated - little Sabbath to examine how well we are feeding his sheep, our neighbors. Sabbaths should have a different fragrance, a slower pace, even if it is simply a short Sabbath during a work day. That is one way to be aware and to feel his presence in the hours of the day. Once again how we pray is how we live and how we live is how we pray.

Take Sabbaths, try to live simply by removing clutter and not replace the old clutter with another variety of trash. Fast by letting something go that really does not aid or enhance our commitment to living prayer. Ask ourselves do I really need to be doing what I am? Can I spend this time in words, silence and action with and for him?

From early childhood until the present time of our living we have been given the gift of many channels and instruments, those special people who guide, nurture and support us. God knows us and knows just the people we will listen to and learn from. Sometimes we do not even realize how blessed we are to be given such a person and then one day the light comes on and we cannot but say, "Thanks be to God!"

Jesus prayed over and over again as he was teaching us. Even up to his final breath he was teaching us to pray. When he rode into Jerusalem on a borrowed donkey, he wept. Tears can be prayer. This was a prayer of sorrow, frustration and disappointment. We have tears that express our feelings far more than any words we can share with God or our neighbor who needs compassion. We may frequently tell a friend or even an acquaintance that we prayed for them, but we can also say I wept for you and those tears were deep, deep prayers. In the upper room Jesus prayed that we would come to his feast and remember him. Yes, each time we claim these words of "take, eat" and "take, drink" in remembrance of me, these words are prayer. In the garden of Gethsemane once again prayers full of tears, but through those tears of painful surrender came that deep peace of shalom. Did the prayers stop then? No, they continued even from the cross. Prayers teaching us to forgive, care for one another, to thirst to share the message and yes at times we would feel abandoned, but in the end we will have run the race through prayer and we too can say, "It is finished" and he will receive our spirit.

I work with groups of people who believe they need to "grow" their life of prayer. After a period of time they are somewhat on their own to use what they have gleaned and to hopefully grow into a deeper understanding and appreciation of living a life of living prayer. At the conclusion of the formal classes it is usually admitted that they had not been satisfied or fulfilled with their prayer life, so they enrolled in the Prayer Seminary. They began by calling prayer a prayer life, but now it is voiced as a life of prayer. There is a huge difference in a prayer life and a life of prayer. We tend to divide our LIFE into categories; we have our home and family life, our work life, our church life and yes, our prayer life. Praying is not one part of our living, it is the whole package. It is not a prayer life, it is a life of prayer, unceasing in all we do, say and think.

As I mentioned previously I have been spending time at the Priory of Saint Scholastica and Monastery of Saint Mary in Petersham, Massachusetts. They live a life of prayer, even it is different from the life of prayer we live it is what they are called to commit to and follow. We are called to commit to and follow a life of prayer, unceasing prayer that is as triune as theirs. It is a life of living prayer through words, silence and action.

Living here for the past months I came to realize that I was living a triune life of prayer through words, silence and action. I spent time in my room alone pondering, reading and writing, time in the common areas communing with other guests and time with the Brothers and Sisters in liturgy and dialogue. All of which is prayer that brought me closer to the trinity, the Father, Son and Holy Spirit.

We had the Father, we needed the Son and we need the power and energy of the Holy Spirit to keep us feeding the sheep and ministering to one another. I needed this time with the religious order to step back and have a very long examining and contemplative Sabbath. The praying people that have come to the prayer seminary knew they needed not just a prayer life, but a life of prayer. It is a journey, it is a pilgrimage and it is a symbol of who we are - disciples of Jesus the Christ!

Even after his resurrection he continued to teach us through his words and actions of prayer. Jesus spoke to Mary and asked her why she was crying – a prayer of compassion, he broke bread, ate and shared fish and told his disciples to carry on the work he had begun a prayer of love your neighbor, feed them not only food for the body but for the soul as well. He also affirmed that they would not be alone and that he through the Holy Spirit would be with them, us until the end of time, a prayer of commitment, assurance and faithfulness.

He not only taught his disciples to pray "Our Father who art in heaven..." but how to pray through living, how to pray unceasingly. He, the humble baby born in Bethlehem, is our Christ, our Teacher our supreme Example. He did not have a prayer life, he had a life of living prayer.

Each evening at the priory and monastery the bell rings at 7:55 for all to gather for the final hour of the day, Compline. The liturgy is prayed and it is time to feel the washing of deep peace and to go out into the night, keeping the great silence.

The day is ended with a prayer of silence, listening for your "still small voice" that has been heard throughout the ages when humankind has listened. Unceasing prayer through words, silence and action is also his presence showing forth profound joy, deep peace - shalom and abiding love.

These pages are my unceasing prayer
of words, silence and action.
May all who read and ponder these heartfelt prayers
Respond to the call of a life of living prayer
through his great and abiding love.

Amen.